THE PASSAGE

poems by

Effie Pasagiannis

Finishing Line Press
Georgetown, Kentucky

THE PASSAGE

Publisher: Leah Huete de Maines

Editor: Christen Kincaid

Cover Art: "Le Passage," copyright 2022 Estate of Kay Sage / Artists Rights
Society (ARS), New York

Author Photo: Effie Pasagiannis

Cover Design: Elizabeth Maines McCleavy

Order online: www.finishinglinepress.com
also available on amazon.com

Author inquiries and mail orders:
Finishing Line Press
PO Box 1626
Georgetown, Kentucky 40324
USA

Table of Contents

The Passage

Is she looking at a sea of concrete,
a sea of glass,
of gleaming gold,
reflecting her long side-swept mane?

Is it a sea of eggshells,
a million and one
fragments
of self, fragile?

I see her from afar,
a landscape foreign and familiar,
I can tell she is thinking like me,
of prisons

What can we do with
all this abyss abysmal
and seductive?
She is wondering like me,

how to create
certainty, surety,
safety
where there are no guarantees

The choices before her:
stay captured and held
drunk with
sensuous vision, or

leap forward
into the unknowable

Figure

hers,
supine
standing sinuous
soft
silk to the eye
supple
sonorous and sad
sculpting grief
into seductive
melancholy,
hers,
full and complete
needing of nothing
no one,
hers,
a satin sash
wrapped around
skin of
her own hand's making
holding her
beautiful inside
in certainty,
hers,
in her lithe vine
of a self,
hers,
surreptitiously
mocking everything
into existence,
shattering the senses
as she moves
with all movement,
hers

Jacarandas

As a little girl
I learned language
the way I later learned
about the honeybees
coming into and falling out of the
ferned tip of my tongue's desire

I had many governesses
but one spoke to me
of Jacarandas so vivid
I dreamt of purple tears
dropping into the Tagus
trapping conquistadors
trying to cross the oceans

T e m p o   a p o s   T e m p o

She spoke to me
of gliding time
and the loyalty of those
Jacarandas standing against
a backdrop of
exiting lovers at dawn

I could never paint those
impossible trees—
I remember them too well,
I know them to be perfect.

The Remembered Self

What did I know then
of the cactus cutting its own skin
to breathe in the lilac
or the Joshua tree
having suffered a long winter
curling in and bowing out

I knew very little of so much
despair unfolding out of reach
and what was out of reach
was unknowable then

yet still I recall so very much
of movement, touch on me,
wet silk clinging round my thighs
condensed novels of joy you
whispered along the edges of
our saffron moment

there was too much beauty beyond
those bay windows of exist,
unbearable witness to all that would go wrong
indoors, and yet we persisted, as I recall

you and I, even during the dusk of
summer when soon all would be
denuded and laid bare,
as summers often are,
we persisted even after we knew of all that
would weather and fade out

Premonition

Remember Yves,
that night we came home
opened the door to find
a wild bird fluttering about?

Remember my screams?
primal, you said
Remember how I pleaded
and pleaded for you not to be
the savior, seafaring savior,
like your father was
a long time ago

I remember your stare—
cold, dismissive
always admonishing me
as a foolish child
I remember you went back in
fought an entire hour
with that winged beast

After, I found the claw marks
on the foyer console
the droppings
on our beautiful
maple floors
and the image of you
opening the front door
shhing my shrieks
as you tossed it back out
into the beckoning night,
a night like a desperate mother
pleading for her missing child

Remember Yves, I dreamt
of many birds that night,
heavy stones,
hanging from live wires
attached to scaffolding
we called home?

how I cried
and asked you to hold me
and never let me go?

Remember how I cried Yves?
I knew all along
the wild bird was you
the wild bird was you

That Instant

After the war
we walked out of
bunkers and
fronts,
sideways
under the panoply
of torn fabric
of what was once
a bridge
holding it all
together
us included

Muted skies,
a khaki tapestry
over our lives,
not a photograph
not a map
in sight to
help us
recalibrate
and recreate

All that hero worship
was it worth it?

We wanted to ask
the sky,
the one that kept our
dark in tact,
a sky
so desolate,
a sky
that kept us walking
robotic and
raw

We were given
no such
answers,
so in that instant

we accepted
all loss
in silence
as we walked
aimlessly,
receding
waning
into the dark

Some
crossed an ocean,
like we did,
with a suitcase
of grief
hoping
we would find
a canvas and
some paints
on the other side -

America,
we crossed that ocean
blind

Automaton

Painted red
bleeding into
a landscape
pastoral
American
weaving
circular rhythms
figure 8s
fire forested
roots reversed
as if they had something
to say about all this
blackened
blots
blotches as if
from ink
footprints
ghastly humanoid
moth wing imprints
on canvas
recording of yet
one more devastation
foundations obscured
they are only props after all
against the forces of this
dark metamorphosis
against our own absurdity

Town Farm Road

I thought it would be enough
to build what we lost
here, for you

A long linear road,
journey of joy and
hope uninterrupted, for you

A former stone home on a farm,
a chestnut fence,
streams running clear, all for you

Open patches of land, no stories of war
under the overgrowth here,
verdant wildflower, the wind spreading it just for you

A forested landscape of white pine and oak,
thick melody of sugar maple, beech, and yellow birch
sheltering you in the shade, all this for you

the tiniest of ripples in our pond,
light fractals capturing the flight
of the robin in the spring,

yet your sighs steal the moment from us,
all too silent and contained, too stale
on this farm road for you, the path not muddied enough,

the water not muddled enough
the shadow the light casts on the curtains
not morbid enough

You and I will never meet here it seems
not even in our afternoon lovemaking,
grown infrequent with each dusk,

you say you are tired, the sun sets too early
casting the faintest pink light
on the white shingled frame of this home now

on Town Farm Road,
your canvas stands blank searing me with guilt,
my idyll was never yours

Of White Flags and Unicorns

Muted shades of taupe and
greys, tattered remnants
of curtains that once
lapped in the wind then
tangled up
outside our windowed frames.
I, the recluse subdued by
You, the warrior drunk;
our definition of peace.
But now the fabric
unravels into a flag
white spiraling
open
I gift it to you.
These days,
I have stopped painting
industrial monoliths
blocking
your passage.
I have picked up
my heavy brush
and dipped it into
blues to paint your waters
clear
in the distance.
This landscape
breathes
and calls to me.
I come quietly
to cleanse you.

Egg

I grew up being told
I was too fragile for my own good,
that word staying with me like
two stuck-together pages in my
favorite book

f r a g i l e

I often searched for definitions
and landed on synonyms
like delicate
slite
weakly
shatterable,
I think delicate and
shatterable
were my words,
almost there
but not quite,
lingering in
liminal spaces,
those I've come to inhabit
with a marked desire
for something,
not being able
to articulate what that
something is,
perhaps missing
entrances I've never
made,
possibilities
of cradling
fragments of an
unfamiliar self

Lately I've come to think of
another word,
one I've been avoiding,

infertile

incapable of
giving
birth,
incapable of
offering
life,
incapable of
inhabiting space for
another
Instead, I've made
this homestead
my womb
you, my project
I wonder where
I'll be when
I've exhausted
all such words,
when I can't
find meaning
in the familiar
I've done everything
not to be shattered
by loss,
everything not to
inhabit inhospitable
worlds,

failing to realize
till now that
I've lived in utter

absence

I've been broken from the start

A History of Unreason

Like an invisible toxic fog
it came over us

songs about being sown
and spent

and something forgetting us
so perfectly

for the last time
hear me, us

like last night's
shadow

bruised over our city
don't look now

blind like before
riddled beings, we are

taking it all in
leaving nothing

but myths behind
the perfect fall

for heaving smiles,
the perfect lies for

speech free like a
lipstick drone

Can   you   taste it?

come with me it sings
walk the faster lane

among shrapnel
on midnight streets

we break bone
spending it all

human flesh,
a blistering wrecking-ball

failing me failing you
our blood lines

a promise of let-downs
and can't hear you's

over the ages of unreason
we overlap

The Answer Is No

Collections of canvases
blocking my way forward
multiplying
yours, mine
by the thousands

canvases detaching
from their frames
leaving splinters
of hurt
on their way out

Retinal detachment,
the doctor tells me,
as if a diagnosis
must be named
to be believed

No, he says
we can't operate this time
I ask and
No it is over and over
and over again

Canvases multiplying
blankness
by the thousands
my vision a void
obliterating me

like your artist friends'
words had -
caustic,
they defined me
as they journeyed to the top

My sex was, like my eyes are now,
an emphatic black hole of a No -
a void
signing me off as
expendable, like Breton
your dear friend had once said of me

I was
always the imposter
of the group
in the move-*amoureuse*
Surrealism

I, the unbidden guest in their sanctum,
at least then, I had my eyes
to see the void
up ahead
and counter it

with the drollness
I chose to embody
or the bleakness
I inked as
my bequest

Choice is lacking on canvases
multiplying blankness now,
blocking my way forward,
by the thousands, a definitive No,
so I gift myself the letting go -

my singular release,
such sweet swiftness
the only note I leave behind -
my words
for you:

The first painting by Yves that I saw, before I knew him, was called 'I'm Waiting for You.'

I've come.

The Conjuror

I'm not able
to imagine the before
only the after is real since
you left me at midnight
I'm a hostage self
Unable to conjure up
plains receding into
distant horizons or
veiled dueling figures
tentative in mid flight
I'm a shrouded lattice
even when the dim
light of the outside
warms its way in to
the back room
filtering through
screened doors
brushing me with
its illusory gleam
Nothing can reach me.
I can make out a tall
ladder leading to some
place I can't see
I can try climbing
but each time
my hands turn
to corrugated daggers
(there is nothing to hold)
You won't find me here
even if you called out my
name
Je n'existe pas.

Go as a River

Lightly I float
on crystalline surface
daylight pooling
on skin, naked with
a life's worth of
truth

I'm seen
clear to the bottom
replete with all the sky
can hold

Lightly I come
to you
as a river does, with pure intention,
an act so absurd,
even you my dear
would laugh

Surrealism

Here, I am the etched abstract

       reflected on spiral lines

Here, I am the aspirant

       of an immutable hope

Here, I am the reveille

       of the unwounding

Here, I am the distillation

       of a love unbound

Effie Pasagiannis is a Greek-American lawyer and writer based in New York City. Her poems have been published in various journals and anthologies such as *Snapdragon Journal, The Write Launch, Platform Review, Anti-Heroin Chic, the Raw Art Review, Fieldfare* Issue 3, *Pen + Brush In Print* Issue 1, and Stanford University's Mantis Press (*Poetry & Protest*, April 2019).

Anagnorisis (Greek: "Recognition"), published by Dancing Girl Press in 2020, is Effie's first collection of poems focusing on universal themes of loss, alienation, struggle and transcendence. The book can be found via the publisher's website and at Book Culture, an indie bookstore in NYC. Effie just completed two poetry chapbooks, *Our Perfect Offering* (a collection of villanelle poems) forthcoming by Dancing Girl Press in 2023, and *The Passage* (inspired by the life and paintings of American surrealist Kay Sage) forthcoming by Finishing Line Press in 2023. She is also writing a collection of short stories with female protagonists at a crossroads. One of these short stories, "Sweet Nothings of a Foreign Exchange," was published in *Feminine Collective*'s September 2018 issue. Another short story, "Fennec Fox on the Promontory," is being adapted into a feature length film by Nomadis Images.

Effie has performed in New York City venues including the Bowery Poetry Club, Arlo Hotels, The Assemblage, Pen + Brush, Powerhouse Books and Poets House. In February 2020, she curated a poetry micro-event and performed at the opening night of "Occupy Project #1" at the Greek Consulate in New York. Most recently in August 2022, she was invited to read poems with the theme memory in beautiful Elizabeth Street Garden as part of McNally Jackson Books summer poetry series.